MW01644412

THE EVERYDAY DISCIPLE +

# LIFE & LEADERSHIP COACHING FOR CHRISTIANS

PARTICIPANT WORKBOOK

THE EVERYDAY DISCIPLE: LIFE AND LEADERSHIP COACHING FOR CHRISTIANS


Church Sherpa
171 FM 3219
Harker Heights, TX 76548
*churchsherpa.com*

Printed in the United States of America.

# LIFE & LEADERSHIP COACHING FOR CHRISTIANS

## Participant Workbook

| YOUR NAME: |
| --- |
| CONTACT: |
| START DATE: |

# TABLE OF CONTENTS

# FROM THE AUTHOR AND CREATOR OF THE EVERYDAY DISCIPLE

Hello, my name is Stephen, and I am so excited to journey with you over the next 12 months through a system that I've created called The Everyday Disciple. It all started with my desire to grow and develop as a Christian. I have always been a learner, and I was taught early on as a Christian that asking for help isn't a sign of weakness but a sign of wisdom.

The Bible says in Proverbs 15:21-22 that Foolishness brings joy to those with no sense; a sensible person stays on the right path. Plans go wrong for lack of advice; many advisers bring success.

To be honest, everything that works in my life has been the result of many advisors, people who have helped me grow and stay on the right path. As I've grown personally through these coaching and mentoring relationships, I started to coach and mentor others. Over time I started noticing that while personal growth is unique for everyone, there are some waypoints and milestones along the journey that work for everyone, every time.

One thing I've noticed is that many times we struggle to connect growth from one area of our life to another area of our life. As a result, we end up spinning plates and looking like a juggling clown. Eventually, we can't balance it all, and something drops and comes crashing down.

As a result, we win in one area and struggle in another, never really having a cohesive plan and strategy to grow holistically. The Bible teaches us in the book of Thessalonians that we are one person with three parts: spirit, soul, and body. You were created to thrive, but you can't do it apart from God's design.

That's why I created the Everyday Disciple System. It isn't just about what you do but how you think about what you do. The key is knowing God's design and thinking differently about why you do what you do.

The Everyday Disciple™ is a 12-month coaching system designed to guide you step by step through four parts of personal growth: Whole Heart Devotion, Personal Vision, Time Management, and Disciplined Habits. I will walk you through an intentional process that I've used personally and have seen work in the lives of many others. I believe that God has designed you to thrive in every part of life, not just one area.

I look forward to facilitating your journey as you develop as a Christian and leader!

**STEPHEN MARTIN**
*Senior Pastor & Coach*

Stephen Martin

## PART ONE

# WHOLE HEART DEVOTION

SESSION 1

# STARTING WITH THE GREATEST COMMANDMENT

Whole Heart Devotion

## WATCH SESSION 1 VIDEO & COMPLETE STUDY GUIDE

*And you will seek Me and find Me, when you search for Me with all your heart.*
***— JEREMIAH 29:13***

The heart is a metaphor for the ___________________ life.

*God blesses those whose hearts are pure, for they will see God.*
***— MATTHEW 5:8***

Jesus always ___________________ to the heart.

*The people were amazed at his teaching, for he taught with real authority—quite unlike the teachers of religious law.* ***— MARK 1:22***

*"What sorrow awaits you teachers of religious law and you Pharisees. Hypocrites! For you are like whitewashed tombs—beautiful on the outside but filled on the inside with dead people's bones and all sorts of impurity. —* ***MATTHEW 23:27***

*Looking at the man, Jesus felt genuine love for him. "There is still one thing you haven't done," he told him. "Go and sell all your possessions and give the money to the poor, and you will have treasure in heaven. Then come, follow me."*
***— MARK 10:21***

NOTES & THOUGHTS

*"You have heard that our ancestors were told, 'You must not murder. If you commit murder, you are subject to judgment.' But I say, if you are even angry with someone, you are subject to judgment! If you call someone an idiot, you are in danger of being brought before the court. And if you curse someone, you are in danger of the fires of hell.* ***— MATTHEW 5:21-22***

*They kept demanding an answer, so he stood up again and said, "All right, but let the one who has never sinned throw the first stone!" Then he stooped down again and wrote in the dust. When the accusers heard this, they slipped away one by one, beginning with the oldest, until only Jesus was left in the middle of the crowd with the woman.* ***— JOHN 8:7-9***

*"You have heard the commandment that says, 'You must not commit adultery.' But I say, anyone who even looks at a woman with lust has already committed adultery with her in his* ***heart****.* ***— MATTHEW 5:27-28***

Your ____________________ flows from your heart.

*Above all else, guard your heart, for everything you do flows from it.*
***— PROVERBS 4:23***

*Jesus replied, "'You must love the Lord your God with all your heart, all your soul, and all your mind.' This is the first and greatest commandment. A second is equally important: 'Love your neighbor as yourself.' The entire law and all the demands of the prophets are based on these two commandments."*
***— MATTHEW 22:37-40***

NOTES & THOUGHTS

## The Shema Prayer

> ***HEAR***, *O Israel: The **LORD** is our God, the Lord alone. **LOVE** the Lord your God with all your **HEART** and with all your **SOUL** and with all your **STRENGTH**.*
> ***— DEUTERONOMY 6:4-5***

1. Shema / ____________________

> *But don't just listen to God's word. You must do what it says. Otherwise, you are only fooling yourselves.* ***— JAMES 1:22***

2. YHWH / ____________________

> *"I am the Alpha and the Omega, the First and the Last, the Beginning and the End."* ***— REVELATION 22:13***

3. Ahavah / ____________________

> *"The Lord did not set his heart on you and choose you because you were more numerous than other nations, for you were the smallest of all nations! **Rather, it was simply that the Lord loves you**, and he was keeping the oath he had sworn to your ancestors.* ***— DEUTERONOMY 7:7-8***

NOTES & THOUGHTS

a. God's love originates from His own ___________________.

b. God ___________________ to love.

*"For this is how God loved the world: He gave his one and only Son, so that everyone who believes in him will not perish but have eternal life.*
***— JOHN 3:16***

c. We ___________________ to God's Love.

*We know what real love is because Jesus gave up his life for us. So we also ought to give up our lives for our brothers and sisters.* ***— 1 JOHN 3:16***

*We love each other because he loved us first. If someone says, "I love God," but hates a fellow believer, that person is a liar; for if we don't love people we can see, how can we love God, whom we cannot see?* ***— 1 JOHN 4:19-20***

4. Lev / ___________________

a. Your heart is where your thoughts, motives, desires, and ___________________ are.

b. The Heart is where the sin ___________________ is.

*Create in me a pure heart, O God, and renew a steadfast spirit within me.*
***— PSALM 51:10***

NOTES & THOUGHTS

*The heart is deceitful above all things and beyond cure. Who can understand it?* — **JEREMIAH 17:9**

*And I will give you a new heart, and I will put a new spirit in you. I will take out your stony, stubborn heart and give you a tender, responsive heart.* — **EZEKIEL 36:26**

*"What goes into someone's mouth does not defile them, but what comes out of their mouth, that is what defiles them."* — **MATTHEW 15:11**

5. Nephesh / ____________________

   a. Your soul is ____________________. It is your life. Your living, breathing, physical being.

   *If you try to hang on to your life, you will lose it. But if you give up your life for my sake, you will save it.* — **MATTHEW 16:25**

   b. Jesus gives you a new ____________________ that results in a new life.

   *This means that anyone who belongs to Christ has become a new person. The old life is gone; a new life has begun!* — **2 CORINTHIANS 5:17**

   *The thief's purpose is to steal and kill and destroy. My purpose is to give them a rich and satisfying life.* — **JOHN 10:10**

NOTES & THOUGHTS

6. Meod / ____________________

*Love the Lord your God with all your heart and with all your soul and with all your mind and with all your strength.' The second is this: 'Love your neighbor as yourself.' There is no commandment greater than these."* — ***MARK 12:30-31***

*"A new command I give you: Love one another. As I have loved you, so you must love one another. By this everyone will know that you are my disciples, if you love one another."* — ***JOHN 13:34-35***

*I don't mean to say that I have already achieved these things or that I have already reached perfection. But I press on to possess that perfection for which Christ Jesus first possessed me. No, dear brothers and sisters, I have not achieved it, but I focus on this one thing: Forgetting the past and looking forward to what lies ahead, I press on to reach the end of the race and receive the heavenly prize for which God, through Christ Jesus, is calling us.* — ***PHILIPPIANS 3:12-14***

NOTES & THOUGHTS

## REFLECT & WRITE

Reflect on what you've just learned. Then, in your own words, restate what you've learned below. Be sure to write down any questions to ask or thoughts that come to mind.

## SESSION 2

# RETURNING TO AN AUTHENTIC FAITH

Whole Heart Devotion

## WATCH SESSION 2 VIDEO & COMPLETE STUDY GUIDE

*Jesus replied, "'You must love the Lord your God with all your heart, all your soul, and all your mind.' This is the first and greatest commandment. A second is equally important: 'Love your neighbor as yourself.' The entire law and all the demands of the prophets are based on these two commandments." —* ***MATTHEW 22:37-40***

__________________ - a set of rules that must be followed to have a good relationship with God.

### Six Forms Of Toxic Religion

1. __________________ religious activity
2. __________________ and Laziness
3. __________________ upon God
4. Manipulation and __________________
5. Extreme __________________
6. Chasing __________________

NOTES & THOUGHTS

## How To Return To An Authentic Faith

*So Christ has truly set us free. Now make sure that you stay free, and don't get tied up again in slavery to the law.* ***— GALATIANS 5:1***

1. Stay in God's Word ___________________

*Your word is a lamp to guide my feet and a light for my path.* ***— PSALM 119:105***

2. Serve others when you don't ___________________ like it.

*"You are the light of the world—like a city on a hilltop that cannot be hidden.* ***— MATTHEW 5:14***

3. Focus on God's work in ___________________.

*"And why worry about a speck in your friend's eye when you have a log in your own? How can you think of saying to your friend, 'Let me help you get rid of that speck in your eye,' when you can't see past the log in your own eye? Hypocrite! First get rid of the log in your own eye; then you will see well enough to deal with the speck in your friend's eye.* ***— MATTHEW 7:3-5***

NOTES & THOUGHTS

## REFLECT & WRITE

Reflect on what you've just learned. Then, in your own words, restate what you've learned below. Be sure to write down any questions to ask or thoughts that come to mind.

# COACHING CALL #1

**Grade the last 2-4 weeks.**

| Circle Answer: | A | B | C | D | F |
|---|---|---|---|---|---|

Think about the last two weeks... Describe any highs, lows, memorable moments, lessons learned, regrets, problems, successes, areas of concern, etc. How are you winning? Where are you struggling?

What would you like to focus on or talk about?

## COACHING CALL NOTES

Record any notes, questions, comments, or thoughts from your call here:

SESSION 3

# CHANGING THE WAY YOU THINK

**Whole Heart Devotion**

# WATCH SESSION 3 VIDEO & COMPLETE STUDY GUIDE

*__Hear__, O Israel: The __Lord__ is our God, the Lord alone. __Love__ the Lord your God with all your __heart__ and with all your __soul__ and with all your __strength__.*
***— DEUTERONOMY 6:4-5***

*Jesus replied, "'You must love the Lord your God with all your heart, all your soul, and all your __mind__.' This is the first and greatest commandment. A second is equally important: 'Love your neighbor as yourself.' The entire law and all the demands of the prophets are based on these two commandments."*
***— MATTHEW 22:37-40***

*"'Love the Lord your God with all your heart and with all your soul and with all your __mind__ and with all your __strength__.' The second is this: 'Love your neighbor as yourself.' There is no commandment greater than these."* ***— MARK 12:30-31***

*"And so, dear brothers and sisters, I plead with you to give your bodies to God because of all he has done for you. Let them be a living and holy sacrifice—the kind he will find acceptable. This is truly the way to worship him. Don't copy the behavior and customs of this world, __but let God transform you into a new person by changing the way you think.__ Then you will learn to know God's will for you, which is good and pleasing and perfect."* ***— ROMANS 12:1-2***

God transforms your life by changing the way you ________________.

NOTES & THOUGHTS

*"My thoughts are nothing like your thoughts," says the Lord. "And my ways are far beyond anything you could imagine. For just as the heavens are higher than the earth, so my ways are higher than your ways and my thoughts higher than your thoughts."* — **ISAIAH 55:8-9**

*There is a path before each person that seems right, but it ends in death.* — **PROVERBS 14:12**

The way you think leads to ____________________.

*Put on all of God's armor so that you will be able to stand firm against all strategies of the devil.* — **EPHESIANS 6:11**

The way God thinks leads to ____________________.

*The Spirit alone gives eternal life. Human effort accomplishes nothing. And the very words I have spoken to you are spirit and life.* — **JOHN 6:63**

Only a new ____________________ results in a changed mind.

*Jesus replied, "I tell you the truth, unless you are born again, you cannot see the Kingdom of God." "What do you mean?" exclaimed Nicodemus. "How can an old man go back into his mother's womb and be born again?" Jesus replied, "I assure you, no one can enter the Kingdom of God without being born of water and the Spirit. Humans can reproduce only human life, but the Holy Spirit gives birth to spiritual life. So don't be surprised when I say, 'You must be born again.'* — **JOHN 3:3-7**

NOTES & THOUGHTS

*The Spirit of God, who raised Jesus from the dead, lives in you. And just as God raised Christ Jesus from the dead, he will give life to your mortal bodies by this same Spirit living within you.* — ***ROMANS 8:11***

God transforms us from the ___________________ out.

*May God himself, the God of peace, sanctify you through and through. May your whole spirit, soul and body be kept blameless at the coming of our Lord Jesus Christ.* — ***1 THESSALONIANS 5:23***

God changes the way you think through His ___________________.

*The message of the cross is foolish to those who are headed for destruction! But we who are being saved know it is the very power of God.*
— ***1 CORINTHIANS 1:18***

*My prayer is not that you take them out of the world but that you protect them from the evil one. They are not of the world, even as I am not of it.* ***Sanctify them by the truth; your word is truth.*** — ***JOHN 17:15-17***

*For the word of God is alive and powerful. It is sharper than the sharpest two-edged sword, cutting between soul and spirit, between joint and marrow. It exposes our innermost thoughts and desires.* — ***HEBREWS 4:12***

NOTES & THOUGHTS

The way you think results in the way you ________________.

- ________________ is about mastering God.
- True ________________ is about God mastering you.

Spend time reading the ________________ every day.

*Your word is a lamp to guide my feet and a light for my path.* ***— PSALM 119:105***

## Biblical Perspectives

1. ________________ is the eternal word.

   *So the Word became human and made his home among us. He was full of unfailing love and faithfulness. And we have seen his glory, the glory of the Father's one and only Son.* ***— JOHN 1:14***

2. The Bible is one ________________ story about Jesus.

   *All Scripture is inspired by God and is useful to teach us what is true and to make us realize what is wrong in our lives. It corrects us when we are wrong and teaches us to do what is right. God uses it to prepare and equip his people to do every good work.* ***— 2 TIMOTHY 3:16-17***

NOTES & THOUGHTS

3. The Bible teaches us the __________________ and ways of God.

> *"Now listen! Today I am giving you a choice between life and death, between prosperity and disaster. For I command you this day to love the Lord your God and to keep his commands, decrees, and regulations* ***by walking in his ways****. If you do this, you will live and multiply, and the Lord your God will bless you and the land you are about to enter and occupy.* ***— DEUTERONOMY 30:15-16***

NOTES & THOUGHTS

## REFLECT & WRITE

Reflect on what you've just learned. Then, in your own words, restate what you've learned below. Be sure to write down any questions to ask or thoughts that come to mind.

## SESSION 4

# STUDYING THE BIBLE

Whole Heart Devotion

## WATCH SESSION 4 VIDEO & COMPLETE STUDY GUIDE

*"You will seek me and find me, when you search for me with all your heart."*
***— JEREMIAH 29:13***

The condition of our ____________________ dictates the ____________________ of our lives.

*Guard your heart above all else, for it determines the course of your life.*
***— PROVERBS 4:23***

*"The heart is deceitful above all things, and desperately sick; who can understand it?"* ***— JEREMIAH 17:9***

*There is a path before each person that seems right, but it ends in death.*
***— PROVERBS 14:12***

*"My thoughts are nothing like your thoughts," says the Lord. "And my ways are far beyond anything you could imagine."* ***— ISAIAH 55:8-9***

*"For the word of God is* ***alive and powerful****. It is sharper than the sharpest two-edged sword, cutting between soul and spirit, between joint and marrow. It* ***exposes*** *our innermost* ***thoughts and desires****."* ***— HEBREWS 4:12***

NOTES & THOUGHTS

We read the Bible with our __________________, but it changes our __________________.

> *"Don't copy the behavior and customs of this world, but **let God transform you** into a new person **by changing the way you think**. Then you will learn to know God's will for you, which is good and pleasing and perfect."* **— ROMANS 12:2**

> *"Make them holy by your truth; teach them your word, which is truth. Just as you sent me into the world, I am sending them into the world. And I give myself as a holy sacrifice for them so they can be made holy by your truth."*
> ***— JOHN 17:17-19***

Hindsight is twenty-twenty, but so is the __________________.

## Basics of Bible Study

1. Pick a __________________.

2. Interpret scripture with __________________.

> *"If you want to be my disciple, you must, by comparison, hate everyone else—your father and mother, wife and children, brothers and sisters—yes, even your own life. Otherwise, you cannot be my disciple."* ***— LUKE 14:26***

NOTES & THOUGHTS

3. Interpret unclear passages with clear ___________________.

*" In the beginning the Word already existed. The Word was with God, and the Word was God, He existed in the beginning with God. God created everything through him, and nothing was created except through him."* **— JOHN 1:1-3**

*"the Word became human and made his home among us. He was full of unfailing love and faithfulness. And we have seen his glory, the glory of the Father's one and only Son."* **— JOHN 1:14**

4. Ask if the passage descriptive or ___________________.

*"Now King Solomon loved many foreign women. Besides Pharaoh's daughter, he married women from Moab, Ammon, Edom, Sidon, and from among the Hittites."*
**— 1 KINGS 11:1**

*"The king must not take many wives for himself, because they will turn his heart away from the Lord."* **— DEUTERONOMY 17:17**

*Jesus replied "The most important commandment is this: 'Listen, O Israel! The Lord our God is the one and only Lord. And you must love the Lord your God with all your heart, all your soul, all your mind, and all your strength.' The second is equally important: 'Love your neighbor as yourself.' No other commandment is greater than these."*
**— MARK 12:29-31**

5. Read the ___________________ Bible.

*All Scripture is inspired by God and is useful to teach us what is true and to make us realize what is wrong in our lives. It corrects us when we are wrong and teaches us to do what is right.* **— 2 TIMOTHY 3:16**

NOTES & THOUGHTS

The condition of your heart dictates the ___________________ of your life.

## The SOAP Method

1. Start with ___________________.

2. ___________________ what you read.

   **Three things to observe:**
   1. ___________________ & Cultural Context – Who is the audience?
   2. ___________________ Context – What kind of literature is it?
   3. ___________________ Context – What is God saying?

3. ___________________ what you learn.

4. Take a moment to ___________________.

Scripture is God speaking to you. ___________________ is you speaking back to God.

NOTES & THOUGHTS

## REFLECT & WRITE

Reflect on what you've just learned. Then, in your own words, restate what you've learned below. Be sure to write down any questions to ask or thoughts that come to mind.

# COACHING CALL #2

**Grade the last 2-4 weeks.**

| Circle Answer: | A | B | C | D | F |
|---|---|---|---|---|---|

Think about the last two weeks... Describe any highs, lows, memorable moments, lessons learned, regrets, problems, successes, areas of concern, etc. How are you winning? Where are you struggling?

What would you like to focus on or talk about?

## COACHING CALL NOTES

Record any notes, questions, comments, or thoughts from your call here:

## SESSION 5

# RELYING ON GOD'S POWER

**Whole Heart Devotion**

## WATCH SESSION 5 VIDEO & COMPLETE STUDY GUIDE

*While Jesus was still talking to the crowd, his mother and brothers stood outside, wanting to speak to him. Someone told him, "Your mother and brothers are standing outside, wanting to speak to you." He replied to him, "Who is my mother, and who are my brothers?" Pointing to his disciples, he said, "Here are my mother and my brothers. For whoever does the will of my Father in heaven is my brother and sister and mother."* ***— MATTHEW 12:46-50***

*But in fact, it is best for you that I go away, because if I don't, the Advocate won't come. If I do go away, then I will send him to you.* ***— JOHN 16:7***

*"If you love me, you'll keep my commandments. And* ***I will ask the Father, and He will give you another Helper, to be with you forever, even the Spirit of truth****, whom the world cannot receive, because it neither sees Him nor knows Him. You know Him, for He dwells with you and will be in you."*
***— JOHN 14:15-17***

***"I will not leave you as orphans; I will come to you.*** *Yet a little while and the world will see me no more, but you will see me. Because I live, you also will live. In that day you will know that I am in my Father, and you in me, and I in you.* ***— JOHN 14:18-20***

NOTES & THOUGHTS

*"These things I have spoken to you while I am still with you. But **the Helper, the Holy Spirit, whom the Father will send in my name, he will teach you all things** and bring to your remembrance all that I have said to you... Not as the world gives do I give to you. Let not your hearts be troubled, neither let them be afraid."* ***— JOHN 14:25-27***

## What's the Holy Spirit like?

1. The Holy Spirit ____________________ you into God's Family.

   ***The Spirit you received brought about your adoption to sonship.*** *And by Him we cry, "Abba, Father."* ***— ROMANS 8:15B***

2. The Holy Spirit has always been ____________________ you.

   *And when he comes, he will convict the world of its sin, and of God's righteousness, and of the coming judgment.* ***— JOHN 16:8***

   *God decided in advance to adopt us into his own family by bringing us to himself through Jesus Christ. This is what he wanted to do, and it gave him great pleasure.*
   ***— EPHESIANS 1:5***

   *Furthermore, because we are united with Christ, we have received an inheritance from God, for he chose us in advance, and he makes everything work out according to his plan.* ***— EPHESIANS 1:11***

NOTES & THOUGHTS

3. The Holy Spirit is ___________________ you.

*And I will ask the Father, and he will give you another advocate to help you and be with you forever—the Spirit of truth. The world cannot accept him, because it neither sees him nor knows him. But you know him, for he lives with you* ***and will be in you***. ***— JOHN 14:16-17***

*Do you not know that your bodies are temples of the Holy Spirit, who is in you, whom you have received from God? You are not your own; you were bought at a price. Therefore honor God with your bodies.* ***— 1 CORINTHIANS 6:19-20***

4. The Holy Spirit ___________________ us and helps us remember.

*But the Advocate, the Holy Spirit, whom the Father will send in my name, will teach you all things and will remind you of everything I have said to you.*
***— JOHN 14:26***

5. The Holy Spirit helps us ___________________.

*And the Holy Spirit helps us in our weakness. For example, we don't know what God wants us to pray for. But the Holy Spirit prays for us with groanings that cannot be expressed in words. And the Father who knows all hearts knows what the Spirit is saying, for the Spirit pleads for us believers in harmony with God's own will.* ***— ROMANS 8:26-27***

NOTES & THOUGHTS

6. The Holy Spirit helps us become more like ___________________.

*For God knew his people in advance, and he chose them to become like his Son, so that his Son would be the firstborn among many brothers and sisters.* ***— ROMANS 8:29***

7. The Holy Spirit directs and ___________________ us.

*But the Holy Spirit produces this kind of fruit in our lives: love, joy, peace, patience, kindness, goodness, faithfulness, gentleness, and self-control. There is no law against these things!* ***— GALATIANS 5:22-23***

8. The Holy Spirit comes upon you in ___________________ at the right time.

*"But you will receive power when the Holy Spirit comes upon you. And you will be my witnesses, telling people about me everywhere—in Jerusalem, throughout Judea, in Samaria, and to the ends of the earth."* ***— ACTS 1:8***

NOTES & THOUGHTS

## Relying On God's Power

1. We need to ask the Holy Spirit for ___________________.

*When the Spirit of truth comes, he will guide you into all truth. He will not speak on his own but will tell you what he has heard. He will tell you about the future.*
***— JOHN 16:13***

2. We need to ___________________ the fruits of the Holy Spirit in our life.

*"But the fruit of the Spirit is love, joy, peace, forbearance, kindness, goodness, faithfulness, gentleness and self-control. Against such things there is no law."*
***— GALATIANS 5:22-23***

3. We need to pray for the ___________________ of the Holy Spirit.

*Let love be your highest goal! But you should also desire the special abilities the Spirit gives—especially the ability to prophesy.* ***— 1 CORINTHIANS 14:1***

NOTES & THOUGHTS

## REFLECT & WRITE

Reflect on what you've just learned. Then, in your own words, restate what you've learned below. Be sure to write down any questions to ask or thoughts that come to mind.

## SESSION 6

# SEEING YOUR LIFE IN GOD'S PLAN

Whole Heart Devotion

## WATCH SESSION 6 VIDEO & COMPLETE STUDY GUIDE

*Where there is no vision, the people perish... — **PROVERBS 29:18***

***If people can't see what God is doing** [they don't know His vision for them], they **stumble all over themselves;** But **when they attend to what he reveals, they are most blessed.** — **PROVERBS 29:18***

Vision connects your life to ___________________ and ___________________.

### Characteristics of Personal Vision

1. Your vision ___________________ with God.

   *One night Joseph had a dream,... — **GENESIS 37:5***

2. Your vision gives you ___________________ for the future.

3. Your vision gives purpose to your ___________________.

   *When Joseph's brothers saw him coming, they recognized him in the distance. As he approached, they made plans to kill him. — **GENESIS 37:18***

NOTES & THOUGHTS

*Fixing our eyes on Jesus, the pioneer and perfecter of faith. For the joy set before him he endured the cross, scorning its shame, and sat down at the right hand of the throne of God.* ***— HEBREWS 12:2***

*And we know that God causes everything to work together for the good of those who love God and are called according to his purpose for them.*
***— ROMANS 8:28***

4. Your vision always puts God ________________.

*And Potiphar's wife soon began to look at him lustfully. "Come and sleep with me," she demanded. But Joseph refused. "Look," he told her, "my master trusts me with everything in his entire household. No one here has more authority than I do. He has held back nothing from me except you, because you are his wife. How could I do such a wicked thing?* ***It would be a great sin against God."*** ***— GENESIS 39:7-9***

5. Your vision won't happen ________________.

*Some time later, Pharaoh's chief cup-bearer and chief baker offended their royal master.* ***— GENESIS 40:1***

*Pharaoh's chief cup-bearer, however, forgot all about Joseph, never giving him another thought.* ***— GENESIS 40:23***

*Two full years later, Pharaoh dreamed that he was standing on the bank of the Nile River.* ***— GENESIS 41:1***

NOTES & THOUGHTS

6. Your vision is ___________________ bigger than you.

*Joseph's suggestions were well received by Pharaoh and his officials. So Pharaoh asked his officials, "Can we find anyone else like this man so obviously filled with the spirit of God?" Then Pharaoh said to Joseph, "Since God has revealed the meaning of the dreams to you, clearly no one else is as intelligent or wise as you are. You will be in charge of my court, and all my people will take orders from you. Only I, sitting on my throne, will have a rank higher than yours."* **— GENESIS 41:37-40**

7. Your vision ___________________ you.

*God has sent me ahead of you to keep you and your families alive and to preserve many survivors. So it was God who sent me here, not you! And he is the one who made me an adviser to Pharaoh—the manager of his entire palace and the governor of all Egypt.* **— GENESIS 45:7-8**

NOTES & THOUGHTS

## 3 Steps to Developing a Personal Vision

1. Discover the ____________________ of your life.

   *You saw me before I was born. Every day of my life was recorded in your book. Every moment was laid out before a single day had passed.* — ***PSALM 139:16***

2. Determine the ____________________ of your life.

3. Develop the ____________________ of your life.

NOTES & THOUGHTS

## REFLECT & WRITE

Reflect on what you've just learned. Then, in your own words, restate what you've learned below. Be sure to write down any questions to ask or thoughts that come to mind.

# COACHING CALL #3

**Grade the last 2-4 weeks.**

| Circle Answer: | A | B | C | D | F |
|---|---|---|---|---|---|

Think about the last two weeks... Describe any highs, lows, memorable moments, lessons learned, regrets, problems, successes, areas of concern, etc. How are you winning? Where are you struggling?

What would you like to focus on or talk about?

## COACHING CALL NOTES

Record any notes, questions, comments, or thoughts from your call here:

## PART TWO

# PERSONAL VISION

## SESSION 7

# PROCESSING TO MATURITY

**Personal Vision**

## WATCH SESSION 7 VIDEO & COMPLETE STUDY GUIDE

### Three People In Proverbs

1. The ____________________ – Knows what's wrong and doesn't care.

2. The ____________________ – Knows what's wrong and does what is right.

3. The ____________________ – Doesn't know the difference.

### How To Process According To Proverbs

1. Process is how ____________________ interpret what happens to ____________________.

   *The first to speak in court sounds right— until the cross-examination begins.*
   ***— PROVERBS 18:17***

2. Process is a fight for the ____________________.

   *Above all else, guard your heart, for everything you do flows from it.*
   ***— PROVERBS 4:23***

NOTES & THOUGHTS

3. Process is about the ___________________.

*Walk with the wise and become wise, for a companion of fools suffers harm.*
***— PROVERBS 13:20***

4. Process with the ___________________, become wise. Process with the fool, suffer ___________________.

*There is a way **that seems** right to a man, but its end **is** the way of death.*
***— PROVERBS 14:12***

*And this world is fading away, along with everything that people crave. But anyone who does what pleases God will live forever.* ***— 1 JOHN 2:17***

5. Process is about ___________________ not comfort.

*Faithful are the wounds of a friend, but the kisses of an enemy are deceitful.*
***— PROVERBS 27:6***

6. Process brings life or ___________________.

*Death and life are in the power of the tongue; and they that love it shall eat the fruit thereof.* ***— PROVERBS 18:21***

NOTES & THOUGHTS

7. Process is about you and ____________________.

*The fear of the Lord is the beginning of wisdom, and knowledge of the Holy One is understanding.* ***— PROVERBS 9:10***

*And we know that God causes everything to work together for the good of those who love God and are called according to his purpose for them.*
***— ROMANS 8:28***

8. Process is about how you ____________________.

*Fear of the Lord is the foundation of wisdom. Knowledge of the Holy One results in good judgment.* ***— PROVERBS 9:10***

## The Wrong Mindset

1. ____________________ Mindset.

2. ____________________ Mindset.

3. ____________________ Mindset

NOTES & THOUGHTS

## The Right Mindset.

__________________ is in charge; I am in control then others are in control.

> *Don't be misled—you cannot mock the justice of God. You will always harvest what you plant.* ***— GALATIANS 6:7***

NOTES & THOUGHTS

## REFLECT & WRITE

Reflect on what you've just learned. Then, in your own words, restate what you've learned below. Be sure to write down any questions to ask or thoughts that come to mind.

## SESSION 8

# PURSUING BIBLICAL TRUTH

Personal Vision

## WATCH SESSION 8 VIDEO & COMPLETE STUDY GUIDE

*Then God said, "Let us make human beings in our image, to be like us. They will reign over the fish in the sea, the birds in the sky, the livestock, all the wild animals on the earth, and the small animals that scurry along the ground." So God created human beings in his own image. In the image of God he created them; male and female he created them.* ***— GENESIS 1:26-27***

### Hierarchy of Truth

1. ____________________ Truth

*They demonstrate that God's law is written in their hearts, for their own conscience and thoughts either accuse them or tell them they are doing right.*
***— ROMANS 2:15***

2. ____________________ Truth

*And so my judgment is that we should not make it difficult for the Gentiles who are turning to God. Instead, we should write and tell them to abstain from eating food offered to idols, from sexual immorality, from eating the meat of strangled animals, and from consuming blood.* ***— ACTS 15:19-20***

NOTES & THOUGHTS

3. ___________________ Truth

*Get rid of all bitterness, rage, anger, harsh words, and slander, as well as all types of evil behavior. Instead, be kind to each other, tenderhearted, forgiving one another, just as God through Christ has forgiven you.*
***— EPHESIANS 4:31-32***

4. ___________________ Truth

*But if you have doubts about whether or not you should eat something, you are sinning if you go ahead and do it. For you are not following your convictions. If you do anything you believe is not right, you are sinning.* ***— ROMANS 14:23***

The Right Ditch – you ___________________ to Biblical Truth

*But avoid foolish controversies and genealogies and arguments and quarrels about the law, because these are unprofitable and useless.* ***— TITUS 3:9***

*Don't copy the behavior and customs of this world, but let God transform you into a new person by changing the way you think. Then you will learn to know God's will for you, which is good and pleasing and perfect.* ***— ROMANS 12:2***

NOTES & THOUGHTS

The Left Ditch – you ____________________ Biblical Truth.

*Woe to you when all men speak well of you, For so did their fathers to the false prophets.* ***— LUKE 6:26***

*You should know this, Timothy, that in the last days there will be very difficult times. For people will love only themselves and their money. They will be boastful and proud, scoffing at God, disobedient to their parents, and ungrateful. They will consider nothing sacred. They will be unloving and unforgiving; they will slander others and have no self-control. They will be cruel and hate what is good. They will betray their friends, be reckless, be puffed up with pride, and love pleasure rather than God. They will act religious, but they will reject the power that could make them godly. Stay away from people like that!* ***— 2 TIMOTHY 3:1-5***

NOTES & THOUGHTS

### The Dangers Of Secular Ideologies:

1. They oversimply ___________________ issues.

2. They divide and ___________________.

3. They become ___________________.

4. They always ___________________.

> *But if you look carefully into the perfect law that sets you free, and if you do what it says and don't forget what you heard, then God will bless you for doing it.* — ***JAMES 1:25***

NOTES & THOUGHTS

## REFLECT & WRITE

Reflect on what you've just learned. Then, in your own words, restate what you've learned below. Be sure to write down any questions to ask or thoughts that come to mind.

# COACHING CALL #4

**Grade the last 2-4 weeks.**

| Circle Answer: | A | B | C | D | F |
|---|---|---|---|---|---|

Think about the last two weeks... Describe any highs, lows, memorable moments, lessons learned, regrets, problems, successes, areas of concern, etc. How are you winning? Where are you struggling?

What would you like to focus on or talk about?

## COACHING CALL NOTES

Record any notes, questions, comments, or thoughts from your call here:

SESSION 9

# CHOOSING TO BE HONEST

**Personal Vision**

## WATCH SESSION 9 VIDEO & COMPLETE STUDY GUIDE

### The Purpose of the Ten Commandments

1. They order our relationship with ____________________.

2. They order our relationship with ____________________.

3. They point to ____________________.

*"Don't misunderstand why I have come. I did not come to abolish the law of Moses or the writings of the prophets. No, I came to accomplish their purpose.*
***— MATTHEW 5:17***

*Honor your father and your mother so that you may have a long life in the land that the Lord your God is giving you. Do not murder. Do not commit adultery. Do not steal. Do not give false testimony against your neighbor. Do not covet your neighbor's house. Do not covet your neighbor's wife, his male or female servant, his ox or donkey, or anything that belongs to your neighbor.*
***— EXODUS 20:12-18***

NOTES & THOUGHTS

## Commandment 9 - Do Not Lie

1. Lying __________________ the truth.

*But God shows his anger from heaven against all sinful, wicked people who suppress the truth by their wickedness. They know the truth about God because he has made it obvious to them. For ever since the world was created, people have seen the earth and sky. Through everything God made, they can clearly see his invisible qualities—his eternal power and divine nature. So they have no excuse for not knowing God.* ***— ROMANS 1:18-20 18***

2. Lying __________________ the Individual.

*Yes, they knew God, but they wouldn't worship him as God or even give him thanks. And they began to think up foolish ideas of what God was like. As a result, their minds became dark and confused. Claiming to be wise, they instead became utter fools. And instead of worshiping the glorious, ever-living God, they worshiped idols made to look like mere people and birds and animals and reptiles.* ***— ROMANS 1:21***

NOTES & THOUGHTS

3. Lying ___________________ Civilization.

*So God abandoned them to do whatever shameful things their hearts desired. As a result, they did vile and degrading things with each other's bodies. They traded the truth about God for a lie. So they worshiped and served the things God created instead of the Creator himself, who is worthy of eternal praise! Amen. That is why God abandoned them to their shameful desires. Even the women turned against the natural way to have sex and instead indulged in sex with each other. And the men, instead of having normal sexual relations with women, burned with lust for each other. Men did shameful things with other men, and as a result of this sin, they suffered within themselves the penalty they deserved. —* ***ROMANS 1:24***

4. Lying ___________________ Our Relationship with God.

*Since they thought it foolish to acknowledge God, he abandoned them to their foolish thinking and let them do things that should never be done. Their lives became full of every kind of wickedness, sin, greed, hate, envy, murder, quarreling, deception, malicious behavior, and gossip. They are backstabbers, haters of God, insolent, proud, and boastful. They invent new ways of sinning, and they disobey their parents. They refuse to understand, break their promises, are heartless, and have no mercy. They know God's justice requires that those who do these things deserve to die, yet they do them anyway. Worse yet, they encourage others to do them, too. —* ***ROMANS 1:28***

NOTES & THOUGHTS

## Commandment 10 - Do Not Covet

*The LORD detests the use of dishonest scales, but he delights in accurate weights.* — ***PROVERBS 11:1***

1. The act of coveting is ____________________.

*For from within, out of the heart of men, proceed evil thoughts, adulteries, fornications, murders, thefts, covetousness, wickedness, deceit, lewdness, an evil eye, blasphemy, pride, foolishness. All these evil things come from within and defile a man."* — ***MARK 7:21-24***

2. To not covet is to be ____________________.

*Let your conduct be without covetousness; be content with such things as you have. For He Himself has said, "I will never leave you nor forsake you."*
— ***HEBREWS 13:5***

3. To be content is to surrender to ____________________.

*Create in me a clean heart, O God, And renew a steadfast spirit within me. Do not cast me away from Your presence, And do not take Your Holy Spirit from me.* — ***PSALM 51:10-11***

NOTES & THOUGHTS

## Integrity is honesty with:

1. God ___________________.

2. ___________________ Next.

3. ___________________ Third.

> *The **integrity** of the upright guides them, but the unfaithful are destroyed by their duplicity.* — **PROVERBS 11:3**

> *There are six things the Lord hates—no, seven things he detests: haughty eyes, a lying tongue, hands that kill the innocent, a heart that plots evil, feet that race to do wrong, a false witness who pours out lies, a person who sows **discord in a family**.* — **PROVERBS 6:16-19**

## Signs Of Weak Integrity

1. I'm ___________________.

2. Choose my ___________________.

3. It's not my ___________________.

NOTES & THOUGHTS

## How To Strive Towards Integrity

1. Do not accept someone else's ___________________.

2. Take action to resolve issues same ___________________.

3. Be ___________________ to people, especially other Christians.

> *Therefore, as we have opportunity, let us work for the good of all, especially for those who belong to the household of faith.* — ***GALATIANS 6:10***

NOTES & THOUGHTS

## REFLECT & WRITE

Reflect on what you've just learned. Then, in your own words, restate what you've learned below. Be sure to write down any questions to ask or thoughts that come to mind.

## SESSION 10

# SPENDING TIME WITH OTHER CHRISTIANS

Personal Vision

## WATCH SESSION 10 VIDEO & COMPLETE STUDY GUIDE

*Love each other with genuine affection, and take delight in honoring each other.* — ***ROMANS 12:10***

*This is my commandment: Love each other in the same way I have loved you. There is no greater love than to lay down one's life for one's friends.*
— ***JOHN 15:12-13***

We ___________________ a lot of people but are known by few.

*In the beginning God created the heavens and the earth. The earth was formless and empty, and darkness covered the deep waters. And the Spirit of God was hovering over the surface of the waters. Then God said, "Let there be light," and there was light. And God saw that the light was* ***good****. Then he separated the light from the darkness. God called the light "day" and the darkness "night." And evening passed and morning came, marking the first day. Then God said, "Let there be a space between the waters, to separate the waters of the heavens from the waters of the earth." And that is what happened. God made this space to separate the waters of the earth from the waters of the heavens. God called the space "sky." And evening passed and morning came, marking the second day.* — ***GENESIS 1:1-8***

*Then God said, "Let us make human beings in our image, to be like us."*
— ***GENESIS 1:26***

NOTES & THOUGHTS

*They will reign over the fish in the sea, the birds in the sky, the livestock, all the wild animals on the earth, and the small animals that scurry along the ground." So God created human beings in his own image. In the image of God he created them; male and female he created them. Then God blessed them and said, "Be fruitful and multiply. Fill the earth and govern it. Reign over the fish in the sea, the birds in the sky, and all the animals that scurry along the ground."* ***— GENESIS 1:26-28***

*Then God looked over all he had made, and he saw that it was* ***very good****!*
***— GENESIS 1:31***

*Then the Lord God said, "It is* ***not good*** *for the man to be alone."*
***— GENESIS 2:18***

You were created to have community with God and ___________________.

## Spending Time With Other Christians

1. My faith is personal not ___________________.

   *All the believers devoted themselves to the apostles' teaching, and to fellowship, and to sharing in meals (including the Lord's Supper), and to prayer.*
   ***— ACTS 2:42***

2. Loneliness and ___________________ are a choice.

   *"When Adam sinned, sin entered the world. Adam's sin brought death, so death spread to everyone, for everyone sinned."* ***— ROMANS 5:12***

NOTES & THOUGHTS

3. The local ___________________ is more than a place you go to.

*"God places the lonely in families; he sets the prisoners free and gives them joy."* **— PSALM 68:6**

*"I pray that they will* ***all*** *be one, just as you and I are one—as you are in me, Father, and I am in you. And may* ***they*** *be in us so that the world will believe you sent me. I have given* ***them*** *the glory you gave me, so* ***they*** *may be one as we are one. I am in* ***them*** *and you are in me. May they experience such perfect unity that the world will know that you sent me and that you love* ***them*** *as much as you love me."* **— JOHN 17:21-23**

NOTES & THOUGHTS

## REFLECT & WRITE

Reflect on what you've just learned. Then, in your own words, restate what you've learned below. Be sure to write down any questions to ask or thoughts that come to mind.

# COACHING CALL #5

## Grade the last 2-4 weeks.

| Circle Answer: | A | B | C | D | F |
|---|---|---|---|---|---|

Think about the last two weeks... Describe any highs, lows, memorable moments, lessons learned, regrets, problems, successes, areas of concern, etc. How are you winning? Where are you struggling?

What would you like to focus on or talk about?

## COACHING CALL NOTES

Record any notes, questions, comments, or thoughts from your call here:

SESSION 11

# BUILDING HEALTHY RELATIONSHIPS

Personal Vision

## WATCH SESSION 11 VIDEO & COMPLETE STUDY GUIDE

Your destiny is tied to your ___________________.

### Threats To Our Relationships

1. ___________________ Hurt Our Relationships

2. Other ___________________ Hurt Our Relationships

3. The ___________________ Desires to Hurt Our Relationships.

Our Sin – Helps us see the best in our self and the ___________________ in others.

> *Getting wisdom is the wisest thing you can do! And whatever else you do, develop good judgment.* — ***PROVERBS 4:7***

> *Do all that you can to live in peace with everyone.* — ***ROMANS 12:18***

NOTES & THOUGHTS

## Building Healthy Relationships

*But the wisdom from above is first of all pure. It is also peace loving, gentle at all times, and willing to yield to others. It is full of mercy and the fruit of good deeds. It shows no favoritism and is always sincere. — **JAMES 3:17***

1. Wise people are ____________________ people.

*So stop telling lies. Let us tell our neighbors the truth, for we are all parts of the same body. — **EPHESIANS 4:25***

2. Wise people are ____________________-loving people.

*Avoiding a fight is a mark of honor; only fools insist on quarreling.*
***— PROVERBS 20:3***

### Three Responses That Hurt Healthy Relationships

1. ____________________
2. ____________________
3. ____________________

3. Wise people are ____________________ people.

*Let everyone see that you are **considerate** in **all** you do — **PHILIPPIANS 4:5***

NOTES & THOUGHTS

4. Wise people are ___________________ people.

   Most of us are oversensitive to the ___________________ of others.

   > *Intelligent people are always ready to learn. Their ears are open for knowledge.*
   > ***— PROVERBS 18:15***

5. Wise people are merciful and ___________________ people.

   Mercy gives people what they need, not what they ___________________!

   > *Love prospers when a fault is forgiven, but dwelling on it separates close friends.*
   > ***— PROVERBS 17:9***

6. Wise people are ___________________ people.

   > *Neighbors lie to each other, speaking with flattering lips and deceitful hearts.*
   > ***— PSALM 12:2***

NOTES & THOUGHTS

## REFLECT & WRITE

Reflect on what you've just learned. Then, in your own words, restate what you've learned below. Be sure to write down any questions to ask or thoughts that come to mind.

## SESSION 12

# TALKING TO GOD

Personal Vision

## WATCH SESSION 12 VIDEO & COMPLETE STUDY GUIDE

### Jesus And Prayer

1. Jesus ________________ each day with prayer.

   *"Now, in the morning, having risen a long while before daylight, He went out and departed to a solitary place and there He prayed."* — ***MARK 1:35***

2. Jesus got ________________ to pray.

   *"And when He had sent the multitudes away, He went up on the mountain by Himself to pray."* — ***MATTHEW 14:23***

3. Jesus prayed for ________________.

   *Jesus said, "Father forgive them, for they don't know what they are doing"* ***— LUKE 23:34***

4. Jesus ________________ God for things.

   *He walked away, about a stone's throw, and knelt down and prayed, "Father, if you are willing, please take this cup of suffering away from me. Yet I want your will to be done, not mine."* — ***LUKE 22:41-42***

NOTES & THOUGHTS

5. Jesus' Prayers had ___________________.

*"When you pray, don't be like the hypocrites who love to pray publicly on street corners and in the synagogues where everyone can see them. I tell you the truth, that is all the reward they will ever get. But when you pray, go away by yourself, shut the door behind you, and* ***pray to your Father in private. Then,*** *your Father, who sees everything,* ***will reward you****."* ***— MATTHEW 6:5-6***

*"When you pray,* ***don't babble on*** *and on as the Gentiles do. They think their prayers are answered merely by repeating their words again and again. Don't be like them,* ***for your Father knows exactly what you need even before you ask him!****"* ***— MATTHEW 6:7-8***

## The Lord's Prayer

1. We must acknowledge God's ___________________ and ___________________ in our life.

*"Pray like this: Our* ***Father*** *in heaven, may your name be kept* ***holy****"*
***— MATTHEW 6:9***

2. We must align our prayers to God's ___________________.

*"May your kingdom come soon. May your will be done on earth as it is in heaven."* ***— MATTHEW 6:10***

NOTES & THOUGHTS

3. Our prayers must be about ___________________ our will instead of bending God's will.

*"Give us today the food we need."* **— MATTHEW 6:11**

4. Our prayers must be rooted in ___________________.

*"And forgive us our sins, as we have forgiven those who sin against us."*
**— MATTHEW 6:12**

5. We pray against our ___________________ and the plan of the enemy.

*"And don't let us yield to temptation, but rescue us from the evil one."*
**— MATTHEW 6:13**

*Jesus said to his disciples, "If any of you wants to be my follower, you must give up your own way, take up your cross, and follow me."* **— MATTHEW 16:24**

Prayer changes ___________________ before it changes things.

*Seek the Kingdom of God above all else, and he will give you everything you need.* **— LUKE 12:31**

NOTES & THOUGHTS

## REFLECT & WRITE

Reflect on what you've just learned. Then, in your own words, restate what you've learned below. Be sure to write down any questions to ask or thoughts that come to mind.

# COACHING CALL #6

## Grade the last 2-4 weeks.

| Circle Answer: | A | B | C | D | F |
|---|---|---|---|---|---|

Think about the last two weeks... Describe any highs, lows, memorable moments, lessons learned, regrets, problems, successes, areas of concern, etc. How are you winning? Where are you struggling?

What would you like to focus on or talk about?

## COACHING CALL NOTES

Record any notes, questions, comments, or thoughts from your call here:

PART THREE

# TIME MANAGEMENT

SESSION 13

# PLANTING THE FUTURE

Time Management

## WATCH SESSION 13 VIDEO & COMPLETE STUDY GUIDE

**Balance is a myth and ultimately unbiblical, why?**

1. Balance convinces us that we don't have enough ________________.

2. Balance causes us to ________________ our lives.

3. Balance leaves us ________________ in the present.

> *Give me the wisdom and knowledge to lead them properly, for who could possibly govern this great people of yours?* ***— 2 CHRONICLES 1:10***

> *To everything there is a* ***season****, and a time to every purpose under the heaven:* ***— ECCLESIASTES 3:1***

NOTES & THOUGHTS

## The Biblical Alternative to Balance is Season:

1. God has given you everything you need in this ___________________.

2. In every season you only have ___________________ life.

3. You can live each ___________________ fulfilled.

> *Don't be misled—you cannot mock the justice of God. You will always harvest what you plant.* — ***GALATIANS 6:7***

**You reap from the past. You sow to the ___________________.** What you do now is all about your priorities.

> *If you need wisdom, ask our generous God, and he will give it to you. He will not rebuke you for asking.* — ***JAMES 1:5***

## Three Things You MUST Do In EVERY Season

1. ___________________ your season – be ___________________.

2. ___________________ your season – change your ___________________.

3. ___________________ your season – adjust your ___________________.

NOTES & THOUGHTS

## REFLECT & WRITE

Reflect on what you've just learned. Then, in your own words, restate what you've learned below. Be sure to write down any questions to ask or thoughts that come to mind.

## SESSION 14

# SEARCHING FOR WISDOM

Time Management

## WATCH SESSION 14 VIDEO & COMPLETE STUDY GUIDE

*No man can belong to two masters, either he will attach himself to one and make light of the other. You must serve God or Mammon; you cannot serve both.* — ***MATTHEW 6:24***

Mamonas - Aramaic for "__________________"

God is opposed to us trusting in riches __________________ of trusting in Him.

*Jesus sat down near the collection box in the Temple and watched as the crowds dropped in their money. Many rich people put in large amounts. Then a poor widow came and dropped in two small coins. Jesus called his disciples to him and said, "I tell you the truth, this poor widow has given more than all the others who are making contributions. For they gave a tiny part of their surplus, but she, poor as she is, has given everything she had to live on."* — ***MARK 12:41-44***

The person who trusts in money can __________________ give what he will not miss.

It is God's Will that we give AND __________________.

*Choose my instruction rather than silver, and knowledge rather than pure gold.* — ***PROVERBS 8:10***

__________________ is the currency of God.

NOTES & THOUGHTS

## 4 Fundamentals Of Wisdom

1. Wisdom comes __________________ blessing.

    *The Lord formed me in the beginning, before He created anything else. Ages ago I was set up, at the first, before the beginning of the earth.*
    ***— PROVERBS 8:22-23***

2. Wisdom is more __________________ than money.

    *I [Wisdom] have riches and honor, as well as **enduring** wealth and justice....*
    ***— PROVERBS 8:18***

    *And God will generously provide all you need. Then you will always have everything you need and plenty left over to share with others.*
    ***— 2 CORINTHIANS 9:8***

3. Wisdom is the channel of __________________ blessing.

    *Bring all the tithes into the storehouse so there will be enough food in my Temple. If you do," says the LORD of Heaven's Armies, "I will open the windows of heaven for you. I will pour out a blessing so great you won't have enough room to take it in!"* ***— MALACHI 3:10***

4. Wisdom has to be __________________.

NOTES & THOUGHTS

## REFLECT & WRITE

Reflect on what you've just learned. Then, in your own words, restate what you've learned below. Be sure to write down any questions to ask or thoughts that come to mind.

# COACHING CALL #7

**Grade the last 2-4 weeks.**

| Circle Answer: | A | B | C | D | F |
|---|---|---|---|---|---|

Think about the last two weeks... Describe any highs, lows, memorable moments, lessons learned, regrets, problems, successes, areas of concern, etc. How are you winning? Where are you struggling?

What would you like to focus on or talk about?

## COACHING CALL NOTES

Record any notes, questions, comments, or thoughts from your call here:

SESSION 15

# WORKING WITH DILIGENCE

Time Management

## WATCH SESSION 15 VIDEO & COMPLETE STUDY GUIDE

*"For my thoughts are not your thoughts, neither are your ways my ways," declares the Lord. As the heavens are higher than the earth, so are my ways higher than your ways and my thoughts than your thoughts.* ***— ISAIAH 55:8-9***

The way to experience God's blessing is to find out what he blesses and ___________________ IT!

Diligence: the quality of ___________________, being careful in your work, being industrious.

*"Lazy hands make a man poor, but diligent hands bring wealth,".*
***— PROVERBS 10:4***

*"He who is slow in his work becomes poor, but the hand of the ready worker gets in wealth."* ***— PROVERBS 10:4***

NOTES & THOUGHTS

## Working With Diligence

1. Diligence is a ________________ behavior.

   *Lazy people sleep soundly, but idleness leaves them hungry.*
   ***— PROVERBS 19:15***

2. Wisdom and Diligence are two sides of the ________________ coin.

   *But don't just listen to God's word. You must do what it says. Otherwise, you are only fooling yourselves. For if you listen to the word and don't obey, it is like glancing at your face in a mirror. You see yourself, walk away, and forget what you look like. But if you look carefully into the perfect law that sets you free, and if you do what it says and don't forget what you heard, then God will bless you for doing it.* ***— JAMES 1:22-25***

3. Diligence is about ________________ not personality.

   *"The **soul** of the sluggard desires and has nothing."* ***— PROVERBS 13:4***

   People who give in to their feelings and emotions, ________________ do well in life.

4. Diligence gives you ________________.

   *"Diligent hands will rule..."* ***— PROVERBS 12:24***

NOTES & THOUGHTS

5. Diligence ____________________ you how to be a disciple.

> *"...You know that those who are regarded as rulers of the Gentiles lord it over them, and their high officials exercise authority over them. You know that those who are regarded as rulers of the Gentiles lord it over them, and their high officials exercise authority over them."* **— MARK 10:42-45**

NOTES & THOUGHTS

## REFLECT & WRITE

Reflect on what you've just learned. Then, in your own words, restate what you've learned below. Be sure to write down any questions to ask or thoughts that come to mind.

SESSION 16

# AVOIDING TOXIC MINDSETS

Time Management

## WATCH SESSION 16 VIDEO & COMPLETE STUDY GUIDE

*Don't copy the behavior and customs of this world, but let God transform you into a new person by changing the way you think. Then you will learn to know God's will for you, which is good and pleasing and perfect.* — ***ROMANS 12:2***

*There is a path before each person that seems right, but it ends in death.*
— ***PROVERBS 14:12***

### Four Toxic Mindsets

1. An ___________________ Mind Set – The false belief that my success rises and falls on me and I use others when I need them for my success.

*God decided in advance to adopt us into his own family by bringing us to himself through Jesus Christ. This is what he wanted to do, and it gave him great pleasure.* — ***EPHESIANS 1:5***

### Questions To Ask

- Do you struggle believing that God could really save you?
- Do you struggle believing that other's genuine care for you?
- Do you end relationships regularly, you quit them before they quit you?
- Do you often think you can only trust God or have the attitude that it's just you and God?

NOTES & THOUGHTS

2. An __________________ Mindset – The false belief that I can take shortcuts and deserve success without struggle or discipline.

   They couldn't trust God with a __________________ because they didn't expect a __________________.

   > *And being found in appearance as a man, he humbled himself by becoming obedient to death—even death on a cross!* — ***PHILIPPIANS 2:8***

## Questions To Ask:

- Do you have difficulty celebrating others, thinking that you deserved more?
- Do you put your identity in what you do and feel that others always take you for granted?
- Do you think higher of yourself than those around you?
- Do you have difficulty asking for help or coming to a compromise with others?
- Do you hate asking for directions?
- Does it offend you when people ask others for advice instead of coming to you?

NOTES & THOUGHTS

3. The __________________ Mindset – The false belief in a perfect life balance that eliminates all problems and setbacks.

> *Give me the wisdom and knowledge to lead them properly, for who could possibly govern this great people of yours?* **— 2 CHRONICLES 1:10**

> *To every thing there is a season, and a time to every purpose under the heaven.* **— ECCLESIASTES 3:1**

> *If you need wisdom, ask our generous God, and he will give it to you. He will not rebuke you for asking.* **— JAMES 1:5**

## Questions To Ask:

- Do you regularly think that you never have enough time?
- Do you make reactionary decisions instead of calmly asking God for wisdom?
- Do you think that you have to choose between a healthy family and a successful career?
- Do you have a poor attitude about your life and current circumstances?
- Do you think you need something else to be really happy?

NOTES & THOUGHTS

4. A __________________ Mindset – The false belief that If I go faster, I'll go farther and be more successful.

> *So let's not get tired of doing what is good. At just the right time we will reap a harvest of blessing if we don't give up.* — ***GALATIANS 6:9***

> *"But don't begin until you count the cost. For who would begin construction of a building without first calculating the cost to see if there is enough money to finish it?"* — ***LUKE 14:28***

God uses the distance between where we are and where He's called us to __________________ us.

### Questions To Ask:

- Are you frustrated with your current position or season?
- Do you blame others for where you are?
- Do you have difficulty finishing or committing?
- Do you lean on your talent versus taking the time to develop your character?

### You Only Lose Two Ways As A Believer:

You lose when you go too __________________ and when you go __________________.

NOTES & THOUGHTS

## REFLECT & WRITE

Reflect on what you've just learned. Then, in your own words, restate what you've learned below. Be sure to write down any questions to ask or thoughts that come to mind.

# COACHING CALL #8

**Grade the last 2-4 weeks.**

| Circle Answer: | A | B | C | D | F |
|---|---|---|---|---|---|

Think about the last two weeks... Describe any highs, lows, memorable moments, lessons learned, regrets, problems, successes, areas of concern, etc. How are you winning? Where are you struggling?

What would you like to focus on or talk about?

## COACHING CALL NOTES

Record any notes, questions, comments, or thoughts from your call here:

SESSION 17

# EXPLORING PERSONALITY

Time Management

## WATCH SESSION 17 VIDEO & COMPLETE STUDY GUIDE

*To the weak I became weak, to win the weak. I have become all things to all people so that by all possible means I might save some. I do all this for the sake of the gospel, that I may share in its blessings.*
***— 1 CORINTHIANS 9:22-23***

*"The Lord GOD has given Me the tongue of disciples, That I may know how to sustain the weary one with a word. He awakens [Me] morning by morning, He awakens My ear to listen as a disciple."* ***— ISAIAH 50:4***

### DISC Personality Profile

D – ____________________

I – ____________________

S – ____________________

C – ____________________

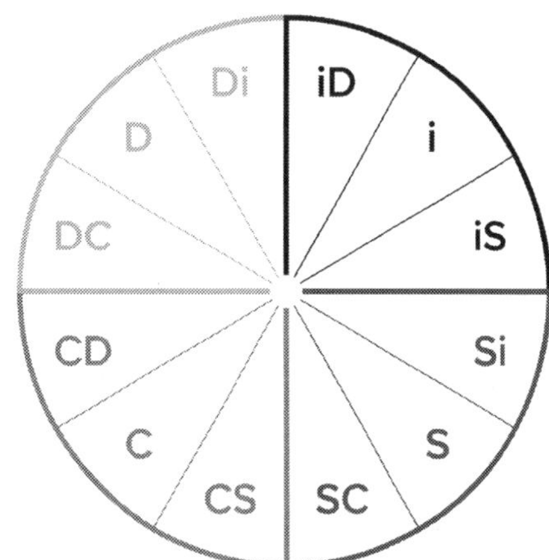


NOTES & THOUGHTS

The profile measures 12 scales (iD, i, iS, Si, S, SC, CS, C, CD, DC, D, Di).

**D - Di, D, DC**
D: measures a direct, dominant disposition using adjectives such as driven, strong-willed and forceful

Di or iD: measures an active, fast-paced disposition using adjectives such as dynamic, adventurous and bold

**iD, i, iS**
i - measures an interactive, influencing disposition using adjectives such as sociable, lively and talkative

iS or Si - measures an agreeable, warm disposition using adjectives such as trusting, cheerful and caring

**Si, S, Sc**

S - measures an accommodating, steady disposition using adjectives such as considerate, patient and soft-hearted

SC or CS - measures a moderate-paced, cautious disposition using adjectives such as careful, soft-spoken and self-controlled

NOTES & THOUGHTS

**CS, C, CD**

C - measures a private, conscientious disposition using adjectives such as analytical, reserved and unemotional

CD or DC - measures a questioning, skeptical disposition using adjectives such as cautious, disciplines and critical

## Three Needs of Every Person

1. ____________________ (value)

2. ____________________ (belonging)

3. ____________________ (approval)

## Four Fears of Every Person

Fear of Losing ____________________ - D

Fear of ____________________ – I

Fear of Losing ____________________ – S

Fear of ____________________ – C

NOTES & THOUGHTS

## REFLECT & WRITE

Reflect on what you've just learned. Then, in your own words, restate what you've learned below. Be sure to write down any questions to ask or thoughts that come to mind.

## SESSION 18

# FAILING FORWARD

Time Management

## WATCH SESSION 18 VIDEO & COMPLETE STUDY GUIDE

*I have told you these things, so that in me you may have peace. In this world you will have **trouble**. But take heart! I have overcome the world."* ***— JOHN 16:33***

### Three Reasons We Fail

1. ____________________ are at fault.

2. ____________________ are at fault.

3. ____________________ is at fault.

*Peter replied, "Man, I don't know what you're talking about!" Just as he was speaking, the rooster crowed. The Lord turned and looked straight at Peter. Then Peter remembered the word the Lord had spoken to him: "Before the rooster crows today, you will disown me three times."* ***— LUKE 22:60-61***

NOTES & THOUGHTS

## Three Stages of Failure

1. The ___________________.

2. The ___________________.

3. The ___________________.

> *When they had finished breakfast, Jesus said to Simon Peter, "Simon, son of John, do you love me more than these?" He said to him, "Yes, Lord; you know that I love you." He said to him, "Feed my lambs." He said to him a second time, "Simon, son of John, do you love me?" He said to him, "Yes, Lord; you know that I love you." He said to him, "Tend my sheep." He said to him the third time, "Simon, son of John, do you love me?" Peter was grieved because he said to him the third time, "Do you love me?" and he said to him, "Lord, you know everything; you know that I love you." Jesus said to him, "Feed my sheep."* — ***JOHN 21:15-17***

## Three Steps To Failing Forward

1. Make a ___________________.

> *And he gives grace generously. As the Scriptures say, "God opposes the proud but gives grace to the humble."* — ***JAMES 4:6***

NOTES & THOUGHTS

2. Move ________________.

*And we know that God causes everything to work together for the good of those who love God and are called according to his purpose for them.* ***— ROMANS 8:28***

3. Keep ________________ forward.

*The godly may trip seven times, but they will get up again. But one disaster is enough to overthrow the wicked.* ***— PROVERBS 24:16***

## Three Church Relationships

1. Every Christian needs a Paul who is ________________.

*Even if you had ten thousand guardians in Christ, you do not have many fathers, for in Christ Jesus I became your father through the gospel.* ***— 1 CORINTHIANS 4:15***

2. Everyone needs a Barnabas who is ________________.

*The news about them reached the ears of the church at Jerusalem, and they sent Barnabas off to Antioch. Then when he arrived and witnessed the grace of God, he rejoiced and began to encourage them all with resolute heart to remain true to the Lord; for he was a good man, and full of the Holy Spirit and of faith And considerable numbers were brought to the Lord.* ***— ACTS 11:22-24***

NOTES & THOUGHTS

3. Everyone needs a Timothy who is ____________________.

*I am writing to Timothy, my true son in the faith. May God the Father and Christ Jesus our Lord give you grace, mercy, and peace.* — ***1 TIMOTHY 1:2***

*So let's not get tired of doing what is good. At just the right time we will reap a harvest of blessing if we don't give up.* — ***GALATIANS 6:9***

NOTES & THOUGHTS

## REFLECT & WRITE

Reflect on what you've just learned. Then, in your own words, restate what you've learned below. Be sure to write down any questions to ask or thoughts that come to mind.

# COACHING CALL #9

**Grade the last 2-4 weeks.**

| Circle Answer: | A | B | C | D | F |
|---|---|---|---|---|---|

Think about the last two weeks... Describe any highs, lows, memorable moments, lessons learned, regrets, problems, successes, areas of concern, etc. How are you winning? Where are you struggling?

What would you like to focus on or talk about?

## COACHING CALL NOTES

Record any notes, questions, comments, or thoughts from your call here:

PART FOUR

# DISCIPLINED HABITS

SESSION 19

# DRESSING FOR SPIRITUAL WAR

Disciplined Habits

## WATCH SESSION 19 VIDEO & COMPLETE STUDY GUIDE

*We are human, but we don't wage war as humans do. We use God's mighty weapons, not worldly weapons, to knock down the strongholds of human reasoning and to destroy false arguments.* ***— 2 CORINTHIANS 10:3-4***

*Finally, be strong in the Lord and in his mighty power. Put on the full armor of God, so that you can take your stand against the devil's schemes.*
***— EPHESIANS 6:10-11***

What you ____________________ with your eyes is not all that exists.

*Finally, be strong in the Lord and in his mighty power. Put on the full armor of God, so that you can take your stand* ***against*** *the devil's schemes. For our struggle is not* ***against*** *flesh and blood, but* ***against*** *the rulers,* ***against*** *the authorities,* ***against*** *the powers of this dark world and* ***against*** *the spiritual forces of evil in the heavenly realms.* ***— EPHESIANS 6:10-12***

*Then the Lord said to Moses, "Why are you crying out to me? Tell the Israelites to move on.* ***Raise your staff and stretch out your hand*** *over the sea to divide the water so that the Israelites can go through the sea on dry ground."*
***— EXODUS 14:15-16***

*The thief comes only to steal and kill and destroy; I have come that they may have life, and have it to the full.* ***— JOHN 10:10***

NOTES & THOUGHTS

## How do you know the enemy is attacking you?

1. Anything that ____________________.

2. Anything that ____________________.

3. Anything that ____________________.

Satan will work ____________________ people, even good people.

> *From that time on Jesus began to explain to his disciples that he must go to Jerusalem and suffer many things at the hands of the elders, the chief priests and the teachers of the law, and that he must be killed and on the third day be raised to life. Peter took him aside and began to rebuke him. "Never, Lord!" he said. "This shall never happen to you!" Jesus turned and said to Peter, "Get behind me, Satan! You are a stumbling block to me; you do not have in mind the concerns of God, but merely human concerns."* — ***MATTHEW 16:21-23***

> *For we do not wrestle against flesh and blood, but against **principalities**, against **powers**, against the **rulers of the darkness of this age**, against **spiritual hosts of wickedness in the heavenly places**. — **EPHESIANS 6:12***

NOTES & THOUGHTS

## 4 Classes of Demons & Evil Spirits

1. "____________________"

*Then the Pharisees went out and laid plans to trap him in his words. They sent their disciples to him along with the Herodians. "Teacher," they said, "we know that you are a man of integrity and that you teach the way of God in accordance with the truth. You aren't swayed by others, because you pay no attention to who they are. Tell us then, what is your opinion? Is it right to pay the imperial tax to Caesar or not?" But Jesus, knowing their evil intent, said, "You hypocrites, why are you trying to trap me? Show me the coin used for paying the tax." They brought him a denarius, and he asked them, "Whose image is this? And whose inscription?" "Caesar's," they replied. Then he said to them, "So give back to Caesar what is Caesar's, and to God what is God's."* ***— MATTHEW 22:15-21***

2. "____________________"

3. "________________________________________"

4. "________________________________________"

*Finally, be strong in the Lord and in his mighty power.* ***Put on*** *the* ***full*** *armor of God, so that you can take your stand against the devil's schemes. For our struggle is not against flesh and blood, but against the rulers, against the authorities, against the powers of this dark world and against the spiritual forces of evil in the heavenly realms.* ***— EPHESIANS 6:10-12***

NOTES & THOUGHTS

## The Full Armor of God

1. The Helmet of Salvation

2. The Breast Plate of Righteousness

3. Girdle of Truth

4. Feet shod with preparation of the Gospel of Peace

5. Shield of Faith

6. Sword of the Spirit

7. Spear of Prayer

NOTES & THOUGHTS

## Three Foundations of Spiritual Warfare

1. The spiritual battlefield starts in your ________________.

   *We demolish arguments and every pretension that sets itself up against the knowledge of God, and we **take captive every thought** to make it obedient to Christ.* — **2 CORINTHIANS 10:5**

2. He who is in you is ________________ than who is against you.

   *But you belong to God, my dear children. You have already won a victory over those people, because the Spirit who lives in you is greater than the spirit who lives in the world.* — ***1 JOHN 4:4***

3. Prayer ________________ more than you think or feel.

   *...The earnest prayer of a righteous person has great power and produces wonderful results.* — ***JAMES 5:16***

NOTES & THOUGHTS

## REFLECT & WRITE

Reflect on what you've just learned. Then, in your own words, restate what you've learned below. Be sure to write down any questions to ask or thoughts that come to mind.

## SESSION 20

# REMAINING PLANTED IN THE LOCAL CHURCH

Disciplined Habits

## WATCH SESSION 20 VIDEO & COMPLETE STUDY GUIDE

*"You are the light of the world—like a city on a hilltop that cannot be hidden. No one lights a lamp and then puts it under a basket. Instead, a lamp is placed on a stand, where it gives light to everyone in the house. In the same way, let your good deeds shine out for all to see, so that everyone will praise your heavenly Father.* ***— MATTHEW 5:14-16***

### Remaining Planted In The Local Church

1. Our faith is personal but not ___________________.

*As Jesus was speaking to the crowd, his mother and brothers stood outside, asking to speak to him. Someone told Jesus, "Your mother and your brothers are standing outside, and they want to speak to you." Jesus asked, "Who is my mother? Who are my brothers?" Then he pointed to his disciples and said, "Look, these are my mother and brothers. Anyone who does the will of my Father in heaven is my brother and sister and mother!"* ***— MATTHEW 12:46-50***

*Jesus replied, "I tell you the truth, unless you are born again, you cannot see the Kingdom of God." "What do you mean?" exclaimed Nicodemus. "How can an old man go back into his mother's womb and be born again?" Jesus replied, "I assure you, no one can enter the Kingdom of God without being born of water and the Spirit. Humans can reproduce only human life, but the Holy Spirit gives birth to spiritual life."* ***— JOHN 3:3-6***

NOTES & THOUGHTS

2. ____________________ is thicker than blood.

*When Jesus came to the region of Caesarea Philippi, he asked his disciples, "Who do people say that the Son of Man is?" "Well," they replied, "some say John the Baptist, some say Elijah, and others say Jeremiah or one of the other prophets." Then he asked them, "But who do you say I am?" Simon Peter answered, "You are the Messiah, the Son of the living God." Jesus replied, "You are blessed, Simon son of John, because my Father in heaven has revealed this to you. You did not learn this from any human being. Now I say to you that you are Peter (which means 'rock'), and upon this rock I will build my church, and all the powers of hell will not conquer it.* ***— MATTHEW 16:13-18***

3. The ____________________ is God's plan for a hurting world.

*"God places the lonely in families; he sets the prisoners free and gives them joy."* ***— PSALM 68:6***

4. The Church is a ____________________ family.

*But Jesus called them together and said, "You know that the rulers in this world lord it over their people, and officials flaunt their authority over those under them. But among you it will be different. Whoever wants to be a leader among you must be your servant, and whoever wants to be first among you must become your slave. For even the Son of Man came not to be served but to serve others and to give his life as a ransom for many."*
***— MATTHEW 20:25-28***

NOTES & THOUGHTS

*All the believers devoted themselves to the apostles' teaching, and to fellowship, and to sharing in meals (including the Lord's Supper), and to prayer. A deep sense of awe came over them all, and the apostles performed many miraculous signs and wonders. And all the believers met together in one place and shared everything they had. They sold their property and possessions and shared the money with those in need.* ***They worshiped together at the Temple each day, met in homes for the Lord's Supper, and shared their meals with great joy and generosity****— all the while praising God and enjoying the goodwill of all the people. And each day the Lord added to their fellowship those who were being saved.* ***— ACTS 2:42-47***

## Six Characteristics Of Spiritual Family:

1. They were fully devoted to ___________________.
2. They were ___________________.
3. They spent ___________________ together.
4. They were ___________________.
5. They were ___________________.
6. They were ___________________.

NOTES & THOUGHTS

*Then Peter said, "Ananias, why have you let Satan fill your heart? You lied to the Holy Spirit, and you kept some of the money for yourself. The property was yours to sell or not sell, as you wished. And after selling it, the money was also yours to give away. How could you do a thing like this? You weren't lying to us but to God!"* ***— ACTS 5:3-4***

*You're no longer strangers or outsiders.* ***You belong here****, with as much right to the name Christian as anyone. God is building a home. He's using us all—irrespective of how we got here—in what he is building. He used the apostles and prophets for the foundation. Now he's using you, fitting you in brick by brick, stone by stone, with Christ Jesus as the cornerstone that holds all the parts together. We see it taking shape day after day—a holy temple built by God, all of us built into it, a temple in which God is quite at home.* ***— EPHESIANS 2:19-22***

NOTES & THOUGHTS

## REFLECT & WRITE

Reflect on what you've just learned. Then, in your own words, restate what you've learned below. Be sure to write down any questions to ask or thoughts that come to mind.

# COACHING CALL #10

**Grade the last 2-4 weeks.**

| Circle Answer: | A | B | C | D | F |
|---|---|---|---|---|---|

Think about the last two weeks... Describe any highs, lows, memorable moments, lessons learned, regrets, problems, successes, areas of concern, etc. How are you winning? Where are you struggling?

What would you like to focus on or talk about?

## COACHING CALL NOTES

Record any notes, questions, comments, or thoughts from your call here:

## SESSION 21

# HONORING GOD WITH YOUR MONEY

Disciplined Habits

## WATCH SESSION 21 VIDEO & COMPLETE STUDY GUIDE

### People Fail For Three Reasons

They are ___________________ – They lack wisdom

They are ___________________ – They lack Diligence

They are ___________________ – They lack Honor.

### Honor

1. Honor is the ___________________ of every meaningful relationship.

2. Honor is the foundation of our relationship with ___________________.

> *Why do you scorn (disrespect) My sacrifice and offering that I prescribed for My dwelling? Why do you honor your sons more than Me by fattening yourselves on the choice parts of every offering made by My people Israel?' "Therefore the Lord, the God of Israel, declares: 'I promised that your house and your father's house would minister before Me forever.' But now the Lord declares: 'Far be it from Me! Those who honor Me I will honor, but those who despise Me will be disdained.'"* — ***1 SAMUEL 2:29-30***

NOTES & THOUGHTS

3. Honor is an issue of the ___________________.

*"'These people honor Me with their lips, but their hearts are far from Me.* ***— MATTHEW 15:8***

4. Honor reminds us that we are ___________________ not owners.

*And He told them this parable: "The ground of a certain rich man yielded an abundant harvest.* ***He*** *thought to himself, 'What shall* ***I*** *do?* ***I*** *have no place to store my crops.' "Then* ***he*** *said, 'This is what I will do.* ***I*** *will tear down* ***my*** *barns and build bigger ones, and there* ***I*** *will store* ***my*** *surplus grain. And* ***I'll*** *say to* ***myself****, "You have plenty of grain laid up for many years. Take life easy; eat, drink and be merry."' "But God said to him, 'You fool! This very night your life will be demanded from you. Then who will get what you have prepared for yourself?' "This is how it will be with whoever stores up things for themselves but is not rich toward God."* ***— LUKE 12:16-21***

5. Honor without a ___________________ is only lip-service.

*And the Lord God commanded the man, "You are free to eat from any tree in the garden; but you must not eat from the tree of the knowledge of good and evil, for when you eat from it you will certainly die."* ***— GENESIS 2:16-17***

*For where your treasure is, there your heart will be also.* ***— MATTHEW 6:21***

NOTES & THOUGHTS

6. Honoring God starts with The __________________.

> *"**I the Lord do not change**. So you, the descendants of Jacob, are not destroyed. Ever since the time of your ancestors you have turned away from my decrees and have not kept them. Return to me, and I will return to you," says the Lord Almighty. "But you ask, 'How are we to return?' "Will a mere mortal rob God? Yet you rob me. "But you ask, 'How are we robbing you?' "In tithes and offerings. You are under a curse—your whole nation—because you are robbing me. Bring the whole tithe into the **storehouse**, that there may be food in my house. **Test** me in this," says the Lord Almighty, "and see if I will not throw open the floodgates of heaven and pour out so much blessing that there will not be room enough to store it. I will prevent pests from devouring your crops, and the vines in your fields will not drop their fruit before it is ripe," says the Lord Almighty. "Then all the nations will call you blessed, for yours will be a delightful land," says the Lord Almighty. **— MALACHI 3:6-10***

Jesus choses to expand His Church to the __________________ that his people honor him.

NOTES & THOUGHTS

## REFLECT & WRITE

Reflect on what you've just learned. Then, in your own words, restate what you've learned below. Be sure to write down any questions to ask or thoughts that come to mind.

## SESSION 22

# MAINTAINING PHYSICAL HEALTH

**Disciplined Habits**

## WATCH SESSION 22 VIDEO & COMPLETE STUDY GUIDE

*Or do you not know that your body is a temple of the Holy Spirit within you, whom you have from God? You are not your own, for you were bought with a price. So glorify God in your body.* — ***1 CORINTHIANS 6:19-20***

*Do you not know that in a race all the runners run, but only one receives the prize? So run that you may obtain it. Every athlete exercises self-control in all things. They do it to receive a perishable wreath, but we an imperishable. So I do not run aimlessly; I do not box as one beating the air. But I discipline my body and keep it under control, lest after preaching to others I myself should be disqualified.* — ***1 CORINTHIANS 9:24-27***

God is the God of the __________________ and the __________________.

*A Psalm of David. The earth is the Lord's, and all it contains, The world, and those who dwell in it.* — ***PSALM 24:1***

*For You formed my inward parts; You wove me in my mother's womb. I will give thanks to You, for I am fearfully and wonderfully made; Wonderful are Your works, And my soul knows it very well. My frame was not hidden from You, When I was made in secret, And skillfully wrought in the depths of the earth;*
— ***PSALM 139:13-16***

You are called to honor God with your __________________.

NOTES & THOUGHTS

*I appeal to you therefore, brothers, by the mercies of God, to present your bodies as a living sacrifice, holy and acceptable to God, which is your spiritual worship.* ***— ROMANS 12:1***

*The Lord says, "I will rescue those who love me. I will protect those who trust in my name. When they call on me, I will answer; I will be with them in trouble. I will rescue and honor them. I will reward them with a* ***long life*** *and give them my salvation."* ***— PSALM 91:14-16***

## 6 Dieting Tips

1. The best ____________________ is the one you will stick with.

2. ____________________ your calories.
   - Caloric Intake = how many calories you take in
   - Caloric Deficit

### Pyramid of Diet Priorities

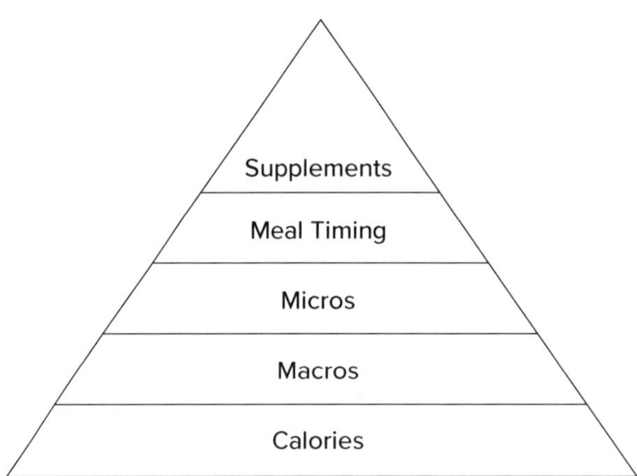


NOTES & THOUGHTS

3. Know how many ___________________ your body needs.

4. Plan your meals in ___________________.

5. Don't take ___________________.

## Recommended Foods

### Protein

- Chicken
- Turkey
- Egg Whites
- Buffalo/Bison
- Whey Protein
- Turkey Bacon
- Extra Lean Beef
- Greek Yogurt
- Fish

### Carbohydrates

- Bread
- Rice/Grains
- Potatoes
- Cereal
- Pasta
- Oats
- Popcorn
- Vegetables
- Fruit

### Fats

- Avocado
- Butter
- Egg Yolks
- Oil
- Olives
- Seeds/Nuts

## 8 Exercising Tips

1. Schedule your exercise in ___________________.

2. Follow a workout ___________________.
    - Lower body, upper body, cardio
    - 4-day training rotation
    - Schedule

NOTES & THOUGHTS

3. Push ___________________.

4. Stay ___________________.

5. Master three basic ___________________.
    - ___________________ Press
    - ___________________
    - ___________________

6. Think ___________________ term.

7. Focus on ___________________.

8. Be content with ___________________.

> *Or do you not know that your body is a temple of the Holy Spirit within you, whom you have from God? You are not your own, for you were bought with a price. So glorify God in your body.* — ***1 CORINTHIANS 6:19-20***

NOTES & THOUGHTS

## REFLECT & WRITE

Reflect on what you've just learned. Then, in your own words, restate what you've learned below. Be sure to write down any questions to ask or thoughts that come to mind.

# COACHING CALL #11

**Grade the last 2-4 weeks.**

| Circle Answer: | A | B | C | D | F |
|---|---|---|---|---|---|

Think about the last two weeks... Describe any highs, lows, memorable moments, lessons learned, regrets, problems, successes, areas of concern, etc. How are you winning? Where are you struggling?

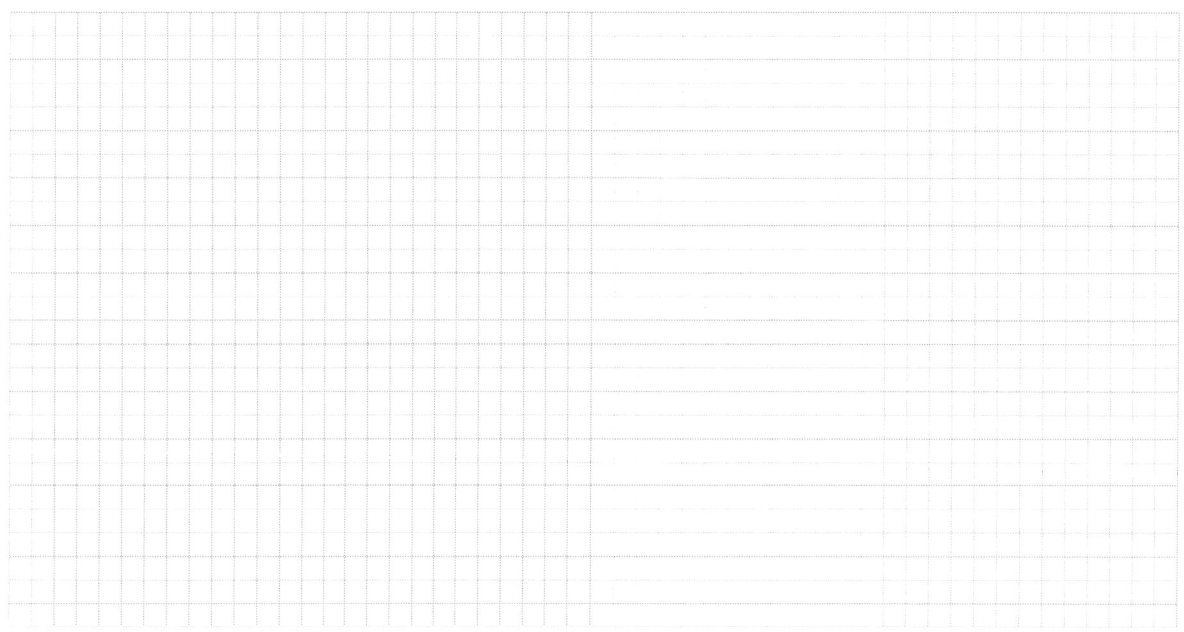

What would you like to focus on or talk about?

## COACHING CALL NOTES

Record any notes, questions, comments, or thoughts from your call here:

SESSION 23

# AVOIDING SEXUAL IMMORALITY

Disciplined Habits

## WATCH SESSION 23 VIDEO & COMPLETE STUDY GUIDE

God is the ___________________ of Love, Sex & Marriage.

### Is it love or infatuation?

1. Infatuation is Based on ___________________. Love is Based on ___________________.

> *"But I say, love your enemies! Pray for those who persecute you!"*
> ***— MATTHEW 5:44***

> *"In the same way, husbands ought to love their wives as they love their own bodies. For a man who loves his wife actually shows love for himself."*
> ***— EPHESIANS 5:28***

> *Love is **patient** and **kind**. Love is not **jealous** or **boastful** or **proud** or **rude**. It does not **demand its own way**. It is not **irritable**, and it keeps **no record of being wronged**. It does not rejoice about injustice but rejoices whenever the truth wins out. Love never **gives up**, never **loses faith**, is always **hopeful**, and **endures** through **every circumstance**." **— 1 CORINTHIANS 13:4-7***

NOTES & THOUGHTS

2. Infatuation seeks to ___________________. Love seeks to ___________________.

> *"This is how we know **what love is**: Jesus Christ laid down his life for us. And we ought to **lay down our lives** for our brothers and sisters."* ***— 1 JOHN 3:16***

3. Infatuation focuses on ___________________ looks. Love focuses on internal ___________________.

4. Infatuation is built on ___________________. Love is built on ___________________.

> *Find a good spouse, you find a good life— and even more: the favor of God!*
> ***— PROVERBS 18:22***

## How to Date God's Way

1. Start ___________________.

> *Do not be yoked together with unbelievers. For what do righteousness and wickedness have in common? Or what fellowship can light have with darkness?*
> ***— 2 CORINTHIANS 6:14***

NOTES & THOUGHTS

2. Test ____________________.

*Whoever walks with the wise becomes wise, but the companion of fools will suffer harm.* ***— PROVERBS 13:20***

3. Guard ____________________.

*Promise me, O women of Jerusalem, not to awaken love until the time is right.*
***— SONG OF SOLOMON 8:4***

4. Avoid ____________________.

*Flee from sexual immorality. All other sins a person commits are outside the body, but whoever sins sexually, sins against their own body. Do you not know that your bodies are temples of the Holy Spirit, who is in you, whom you have received from God? You are not your own; you were bought at a price. Therefore honor God with your bodies.* ***— 1 CORINTHIANS 6:18-20***

*But from the beginning of the creation, God 'made them male and female.' 'For this reason a man shall leave his father and mother and be joined to his wife, and the two shall become one flesh'; so then they are no longer two, but one flesh. Therefore what God has joined together, let not man separate."*
***— MARK 10:6-9***

NOTES & THOUGHTS

## What Is Marriage?

1. Marriage is __________________ plan.

> *"My thoughts are nothing like your thoughts," says the Lord. "And my ways are far beyond anything you could imagine. For just as the heavens are higher than the earth, so my ways are higher than your ways and my thoughts higher than your thoughts.* — ***ISAIAH 55:8-9***

2. Marriage is between one __________________ and one __________________ with God for life.

3. __________________ was designed by God for marriage.

> *"Today I have given you the choice between life and death, between blessings and curses. Now I call on heaven and earth to witness the choice you make. Oh, that you would choose life, so that you and your descendants might live! You can make this choice by loving the Lord your God, obeying him, and committing yourself firmly to him. This is the key to your life. And if you love and obey the Lord, you will live long in the land the Lord swore to give your ancestors Abraham, Isaac, and Jacob."* — ***DEUTERONOMY 30:19-20***

NOTES & THOUGHTS

## REFLECT & WRITE

Reflect on what you've just learned. Then, in your own words, restate what you've learned below. Be sure to write down any questions to ask or thoughts that come to mind.

SESSION 24

# RESOLVING CONFLICT & UNFORGIVENESS

Disciplined Habits

## WATCH SESSION 24 VIDEO & COMPLETE STUDY GUIDE

*"Do not repay anyone evil for evil. Be careful to do what is right in the eyes of everyone. If it is possible, as far as it depends on you, live at peace with everyone."* — ***ROMANS 12:17-18***

### Three Effects of Unresolved Conflict

1. It Hinders Our __________________ with God.

*Whoever claims to love God yet hates a brother or sister is a liar. For whoever does not love their brother and sister, whom they have seen, cannot love God, whom they have not seen.* — ***1 JOHN 4:20***

*There are six things the Lord hates—no, seven things he detests: haughty eyes, a lying tongue, hands that kill the innocent, a heart that plots evil, feet that race to do wrong, a false witness who pours out lies,* ***a person who sows discord in a family.*** — ***PROVERBS 6:16-19***

*Therefore, whenever we have the opportunity, we should do good to everyone—especially to those in the family of faith.* — ***GALATIANS 6:10***

NOTES & THOUGHTS

2. It Hinders Our ____________________.

*"Therefore, if you are offering your gift at the altar and there remember that your brother or sister has something against you, leave your gift there in front of the altar. First go and be reconciled to them; then come and offer your gift."* ***— MATTHEW 5:23-24***

3. It Hinders Our Spiritual ____________________.

*Now these are the gifts Christ gave to the church: the apostles, the prophets, the evangelists, and the pastors and teachers. Their responsibility is to equip God's people to do his work and build up the church, the **body of Christ**. This will continue until we all come to such **unity** in our faith and knowledge of God's Son that we will be **mature** in the Lord, measuring up to the **full** and **complete** standard of Christ.* ***— EPHESIANS 4:11-13***

## The Biblical Way to Resolve Conflict

1. ____________________ first.

*"If another believer sins against you, go privately and point out the offense. If the other person listens and confesses it, you have won that person back. But if you are unsuccessful, take one or two others with you and go back again, so that everything you say may be confirmed by two or three witnesses. If the person still refuses to listen, take your case to the church. Then if he or she won't accept the church's decision, treat that person as a pagan or a corrupt tax collector.* ***— MATTHEW 18:15-17***

NOTES & THOUGHTS

*"I heard you in the garden, and I was afraid because I was naked, so I hid."*
***— GENESIS 3:10***

*"For the Spirit **God** gave us does not make us timid, but gives us power, love, and self-discipline."* ***— 2 TIMOTHY 1:7***

2. ____________________ your part.

*"Why do you notice the little piece of dust in your friend's eye, but you don't notice the big piece of wood in your own eye? First, take the log out of your own eye. Then you'll see clearly to take the splinter out of your friend's eye."*
***— MATTHEW 7:3***

Will you forgive me, I was only thinking of myself?

3. ____________________ for the hurt.

*My dear brothers and sisters, take note of this: Everyone should be quick to listen, slow to speak and slow to be come angry."* ***— JAMES 1:19***

4. ____________________ their perspective.

*"Not looking to your own interests but each of you to the interests of the others. In your relationships with one another, have the same mindset as Christ Jesus."* ***— PHILIPPIANS 2:4-5***

NOTES & THOUGHTS

5. ____________________ the truth in love.

*"The words of the reckless pierce like swords, but the tongue of the wise brings healing."* — ***PROVERBS 12:18***

6. ____________________ on the solution.

*"But now you must also rid yourselves of all such things as these: anger, rage, malice, slander, and filthy language from your lips."* — ***COLOSSIANS 3:8***

7. ____________________ the relationship.

*"For there is one God and one mediator between God and mankind, the man Christ Jesus..."* — ***1 TIMOTHY 2:5***

NOTES & THOUGHTS

## REFLECT & WRITE

Reflect on what you've just learned. Then, in your own words, restate what you've learned below. Be sure to write down any questions to ask or thoughts that come to mind.

# COACHING CALL #12

**Grade the last 2-4 weeks.**

| Circle Answer: | A | B | C | D | F |
|---|---|---|---|---|---|

Think about the last two weeks... Describe any highs, lows, memorable moments, lessons learned, regrets, problems, successes, areas of concern, etc. How are you winning? Where are you struggling?

What would you like to focus on or talk about?

## COACHING CALL NOTES

Record any notes, questions, comments, or thoughts from your call here:

# ANSWER KEY

## PART ONE - WHOLE HEART DEVOTION

**Session One: Starting with the Greatest Commandment**

Page 9 - inner, taught
Page 10 - life
Page 11 - Hear, LORD, Love
Page 12 - character, chooses, respond, Heart, affections, problem
Page 13 - Soul, you, heart
Page 14 - Strength

**Session Two: Returning to an Authentic Faith**

Page 19 - Religion, Compulsive, Apathy, Presumption, Control, Intolerance, Experiences
Page 20 - Daily, feel, you

**Session Three: Changing the Way You Think**

Page 29 - think
Page 30 - death, life, heart
Page 31 - inside, Word
Page 32 - act, Religion, faith, Bible, Jesus, unified
Page 33 - will

**Session Four: Studying the Bible**

Page 39 - heart, direction
Page 40 - mind, heart, Bible, Translation, scripture
Page 41 - passages, prescriptive, whole
Page 42 - direction, Scripture, Observe, Historical, Literary, Theological, apply, pray, Prayer

**Session Five: Relying on God's Power**

Page 52 - adopts, with
Page 53 - in, teaches, pray
Page 54 - Jesus, guides, power
Page 55 - wisdom, recognize, gifts

**Session Six: Seeing Your Life in God's Plan**

Page 61 - signifinance, purpose, starts, hope, pain
Page 62 - first, overnight
Page 63 - always, outlasts
Page 64 - why, what, who

## PART TWO - PERSONAL VISION

**Session Seven: Processing to Maturity**

Page 75 - Fool, Wise, Simple, you, you, heart
Page 76 - who, wise, harm, growth, death
Page 77 - God, think, Control, Victim, Godless
Page 78 - God

**Session Eight: Pursuing Biblical Truth**

Page 83 - Absolute, Principled
Page 84 - Subjective, Personal, add, ditches
Page 85 - reject
Page 86 - complex, conquer, idols, fail

**Session Nine: Choosing to Be Honest**

Page 95 - God, others, Jesus
Page 96 - Denies, Darkens
Page 97 - Denigrates, Destroys
Page 98 - unseen, content, Jesus
Page 99 - First, Yourself, Others, right, side, fault
Page 100 - offense, day, loyal

**Session Ten: Spending Time with Other Christians**

Page 105 - know
Page 106 - others, private, isolation
Page 107 - Church

**Session Eleven: Building Healthy Relationships**

Page 117 - relationships, We, People, Devil, worst
Page 118 - honest, peace, Comparing, Condemning, Contradicting, considerate
Page 119 - reasonable, opinions, kind, deserve, sincere

**Session Twelve: Talking to God**

Page 125 - started, alone, others, asked
Page 126 - power, power, position, will
Page 127 - surrendering, forgiveness, flesh, you

## PART THREE - TIME MANAGEMENT

**Session Thirteen: Planting the Future**

Page 139 - time, compartmentalize, unfulfilled

Page 140 - season, one, day, future, Accept, honest, Own, attitude, Work, priorities

**Session Fourteen: Searching for Wisdom**

Page 145 - riches, instead, only, receive, Wisdom

Page 146 - before, valuable, continual, converted

**Session Fifteen: Working with Diligence**

Page 155 - DO, persevering

Page 156 - learned, same, character, don't, influence

Page 157 - teaches

**Session Sixteen: Avoiding Toxic Mindsets**

Page 163 - Orphan

Page 164 - Entitlement, step, fight

Page 165 - Balance

Page 166 - Speed, develop, fast, alone

**Session Seventeen: Exploring Personality**

Page 175 - Dominance, Influence, Steadiness, Conscientiousness

Page 177 - Affection, Acceptance, Affirmation, Control, Rejection, Security, Criticism

**Session Eighteen: Failing Forward**

Page 183 - We, They, No one

Page 184 - Moment, Pain, Purpose, change

Page 185 - forward, moving, leading, loving

Page 186 - learning

## PART FOUR - DISCIPLINED HABITS

**Session Nineteen: Dressing for Spiritual War**

Page 197 - see
Page 198 - steals, kills, destroys, through
Page 199 - Principalities, The Powers, Rulers of the Darkness of this World, Spiritual Hosts of Wickedness in High Places
Page 201 - mind, greater, accomplishes

**Session Twenty: Remaining Planted in the Local Church**

Page 207 - private
Page 208 - Spirit, Church, spiritual
Page 209 - God, generous, time, joyful, inclusive, exclusive

**Session Twenty-One: Honoring God with Your Money**

Page 219 - foolish, lazy, entitlement, foundation, God
Page 220 - heart, stewards, test
Page 221 - Tithe, level

**Session Twenty-Two: Maintaining Physical Health**

Page 227 - natural, supernatural, body
Page 228 - diet, Count
Page 229 - calories, advance, shortcuts, advance, program
Page 230 - yourself, humble, exercises, Bench, Squat, Deadlift, long, progress, improvement

**Session Twenty-Three: Avoiding Sexual Immorality**

Page 239 - Creator, Feeling, Commitment
Page 240 - be served, sacrifice, external, character, physical, spiritual, Spiritual
Page 241 - Relational, Emotional, Physical
Page 242 - God's, man, woman, Sex

**Session Twenty-Four: Resolving Conflict & Unforgiveness**

Page 247 - Relationship
Page 248 - Prayers, Maturity, Act
Page 249 - Own, Listen, Considerate
Page 250 - Speak, Focus, Value

# ADDITIONAL RESOURCES

## Lasting Change

***A Systems-Based Approach To The Christian Life***
by Stephen Martin

**Sustaining personal growth using eight systems of faith.**

In ***Lasting Change: A Systems-Based Approach To The Christian Life***™ we will explore personal growth using a systems-based approach. By using this approach, we can gain a greater understanding of how various systems of faith work together and how, when implemented into our lives, we can experience sustainable and lasting change. By understanding these faith systems, much like a physician with our physical systems, we will be able to identify, assess and address issues in our Christian life.

## Start Here

*An Introduction To The Gospel, The Holy Spirit And The Local Church*

by Stephen Martin

*Start Here: An Introduction To The Gospel, The Holy Spirit And The Local Church*, is designed to help you jump-start your faith by getting to know God through His Word, the Bible.

With everything surrounding us today, it can be hard to know where to start, especially in regard to following Jesus. Start Here is a 21-day guided devotional where you will learn three essentials that form the foundation of the Christian life: The Gospel, The Holy Spirit and The Local Church. You will spend seven days focusing on each of these essentials as you continue to grow in your faith over time.

## Honest To God

*365-Day Of Personal Devotion*

by Stephen Martin

Grow closer to God each day through intentional personal devotion that prioritizes worship, Bible study, prayer, and community. By following a simple but powerful template, you will grow closer to God and toward His plan for your life.

## Better

***My Life. God's Design.***

by Stephen Martin

**We want "better," and we want it now.**

Americans spend billions of dollars every year in our efforts to get better. We want to be better today than we were yesterday and better tomorrow than we are today. We want next year to be better than last.
We're worried that we're not good enough and, no matter how hard we try, we can never measure up to everyone's expectations. We want to be better people, better friends, better husbands or wives, better parents. We want "better," and we want it now.

But what if the key to "better" isn't what we think it is? What if it doesn't start with us at all?

**What if our concept of "better" isn't good enough?**

With its essential life-application principles and in-depth personal and group study materials, ***Better: My Life. God's Design.*** by Stephen Martin is designed to help you learn the keys to "better" and discover that, with God's help, the better life you want is within your reach.

## Wiser

***How To Build And Manage Wealth God's Way***

by Stephen Martin

**Richer. Winner. Owner. Wealthier. Happier.**

Whenever we think about our finances, those are some of the words that usually come to mind. If you want to be a winner in this world, you need to have a big house, a big car, and a big paycheck. Right? Everyone thinks that having more money and owning more stuff naturally makes you happier in life.

**But what if everyone is wrong?**

What if happiness isn't really tied to the number of things you possess, the size of your bank account, or what you can claim ownership over in this life? What if the key to becoming happier with our personal finances and possessions was found in just one word? ***Wiser***.

Building wealth and leaving a legacy that makes a real impact in this world isn't just about becoming richer. It's about becoming ***Wiser***. It's about understanding four important biblical principles and applying them practically in our lives. As we learn and practice the four foundational truths presented in this book, we'll discover that building and stewarding our resources God's way will bring us true and lasting wealth.

Made in the USA
Columbia, SC
23 December 2022

e777f497-2645-463f-95d8-f55b06916327R01